CELEBRATING THE NAME BRENDA

Celebrating the Name Brenda

Walter the Educator

Silent King Books

Copyright © 2024 by Walter the Educator

All rights reserved. No part of this book may be reproduced in any manner whatsoever without written permission except in the case of brief quotations embodied in critical articles and reviews.

First Printing, 2024

Disclaimer
This book is a literary work; poems are not about specific persons, locations, situations, and/or circumstances unless mentioned in a historical context. This book is for entertainment and informational purposes only. The author and publisher offer this information without warranties expressed or implied. No matter the grounds, neither the author nor the publisher will be accountable for any losses, injuries, or other damages caused by the reader's use of this book. The use of this book acknowledges an understanding and acceptance of this disclaimer.

dedicated to everyone with the first name of Brenda

BRENDA

Melodies dance on the lips of dawn,

BRENDA

Resides a name, a beacon bright, where hearts are drawn.

BRENDA

Brenda, oh Brenda, thy name a symphony untold,

BRENDA

In realms of poetry and prose, its beauty boldly unfold.

BRENDA

In whispers soft as twilight's sigh, Brenda's name doth rise,

BRENDA

A gentle breeze that softly sighs beneath cerulean skies.

BRENDA

Like petals of a rose unfurling in the morning light,

BRENDA

Brenda, oh Brenda, thy name a radiant sight.

BRENDA

In valleys deep and mountains high, where echoes softly roam,

BRENDA

Brenda's name resounds with grace, a melody to call home.

BRENDA

It dances on the river's song, a serenade so sweet,

BRENDA

In every ripple, every note, Brenda's name doth meet.

BRENDA

In fields where golden sunflowers sway with every breeze,

BRENDA

Brenda's name is whispered by the whispering trees.

BRENDA

It lingers in the dappled shade, a secret softly shared,

BRENDA

In every rustle, every hush, Brenda's name declared.

BRENDA

In the tapestry of life's embrace, where stories intertwine,

BRENDA

Brenda's name a golden thread, in every verse divine.

BRENDA

It weaves through laughter, through tears, in every chapter told,

BRENDA

In every heartbeat, every sigh, Brenda's name enfold.

BRENDA

In dreams where stars paint the canvas of the endless night,

BRENDA

Brenda's name a guiding light, a beacon burning bright.

BRENDA

It sparkles in the velvet sky, a constellation rare,

BRENDA

In every twinkle, every gleam, Brenda's name to wear.

BRENDA

In the whispers of the universe, where secrets softly sing,

BRENDA

Brenda's name a sacred chant, a hymn to everything.

BRENDA

It echoes through eternity, a timeless melody,

BRENDA

In every breath, every heartbeat, Brenda's legacy.

BRENDA

So let us raise our voices high, in praise of
Brenda's name,

BRENDA

A tribute to its timeless grace, its everlasting flame.

BRENDA

For in this world of endless change, one thing shall remain,

BRENDA

The beauty of Brenda's name, forever to proclaim.

BRENDA

In gardens where the roses bloom, in hues of red and gold,

BRENDA

Brenda's name a fragrant breeze, a tale of love untold.

BRENDA

It whispers through the petals fair, a song of sweet romance,

BRENDA

In every bloom, every perfume, Brenda's name to enhance.

BRENDA

And when the night descends again, with stars that softly gleam,

BRENDA

Brenda's name a lullaby, a soothing, gentle stream.

BRENDA

It cradles all within its arms, in dreams of peace and rest,

BRENDA

In every slumber, every dream, Brenda's name blessed.

BRENDA

ABOUT THE CREATOR

Walter the Educator is one of the pseudonyms for Walter Anderson. Formally educated in Chemistry, Business, and Education, he is an educator, an author, a diverse entrepreneur, and he is the son of a disabled war veteran. "Walter the Educator" shares his time between educating and creating. He holds interests and owns several creative projects that entertain, enlighten, enhance, and educate, hoping to inspire and motivate you.

> Follow, find new works, and stay up to date
> with Walter the Educator™
> at WaltertheEducator.com

www.ingramcontent.com/pod-product-compliance
Lightning Source LLC
LaVergne TN
LVHW010622070526
838199LV00063BA/5235